Snowcap

Canadian Alphabet

BY
Michael Hong xiang Zhu

B b
is for Banff,
the jewel of the
Canadian Rockies.

C c
is for Canada.
Oh, our great
beautiful country!

Yukon Territory

Northwest Territories

Nunavut

British Columbia

Alberta

Saskatchewan

Manitoba

Ontario

Québec

Newfound

New Brun

Ottawa ☆

F f

is for flag, held up
high in the sky.

I i
is for Inukshuk,
a man-made
landmark.

J j

is for Jasper,
a great place for
summer trips.

K k
is for kayak.
Paddle on!

Nn is for Niagara Falls, the most powerful waterfall in North America.

P p
is for Polar Bear,
who lives in
the Arctic region.

Qq is for Québec City, a French-Canadian City.

These animals are lost !
Can you help them find their homes?

St.John's

Banff

Whistler

Ottawa

T t
is for Toronto,
Canada's largest city
by the Great Lakes.

U u
is for Ucluelet,
a seaside town
on Vancouver
Island.

Vv

is for Vancouver, a city by the Pacific Ocean.

X x

is for X-country skiing, across our snowy fields.

Y y is for Yukon, located in the northwest of Canada.